D1615433

microbes

written and illustrated by amy gallagher

THUNDERSTONE
BOOKS

978-1-63411-009-9 (ISBN 13)

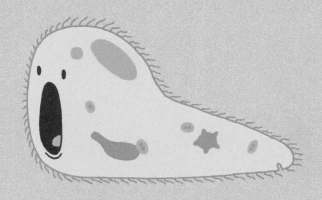

contents

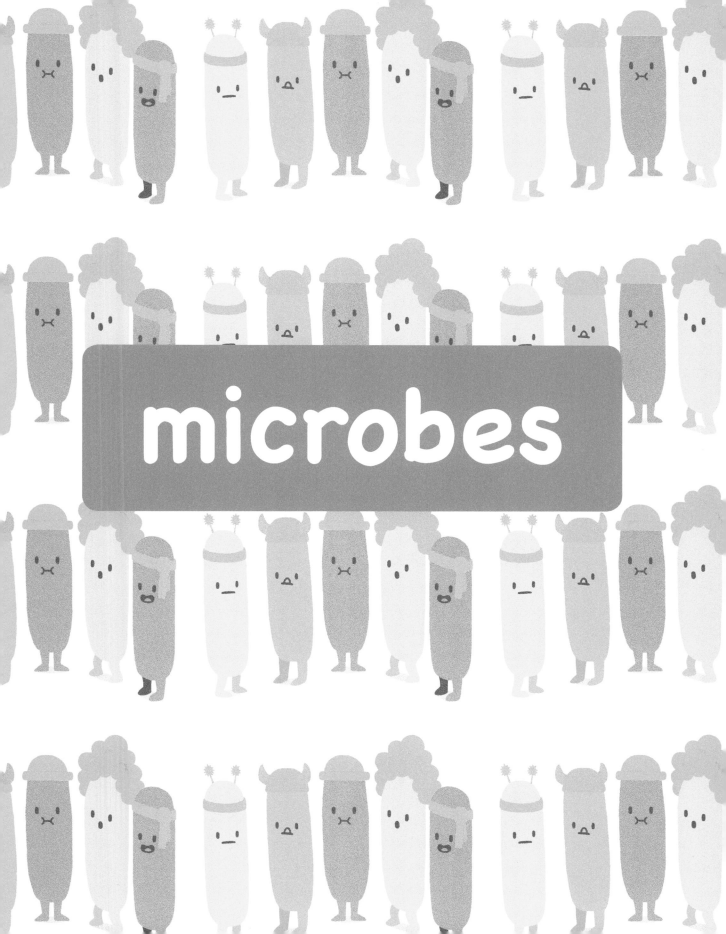

Microbes are incredibly tiny organisms; they are so small that **MILLIONS** of them can fit on a head of a pin. These cells, although invisible to the naked eye, are vital to the human race and the world.

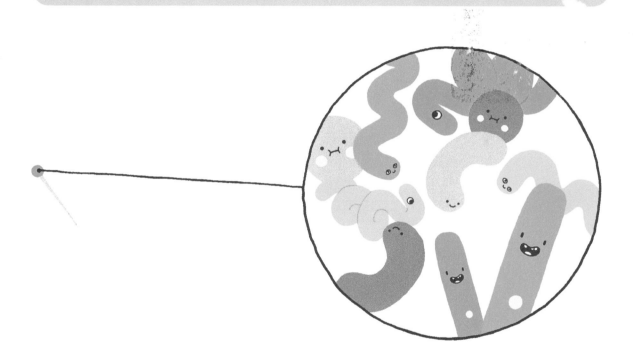

Without microbes we could not eat or breathe, rubbish would not decay, and plants could not grow. They exist **EVERYWHERE**: the ground we walk on, the food we eat, extremely hot and cold environments, even **INSIDE US**!

Microbes have existed for at least **THREE THOUSAND FIVE HUNDRED MILLION YEARS**. Yet one discovery in northwest Australia suggests a type of bacteria to have existed **THREE BILLION FIVE HUNDRED MILLION YEARS AGO**! (That's **BEFORE** oxygen!)

Microbes are better known for the diseases they cause, but there are microbes that are beneficial to us. For example, yeast cells are used to help bread rise and ferment food to make alcohol.

This book will introduce you to six types of microbes including **FUNGI**, **BACTERIA**, **VIRUSES**, **ALGAE**, **ARCHAEA**, **AND PROTOZOA**.

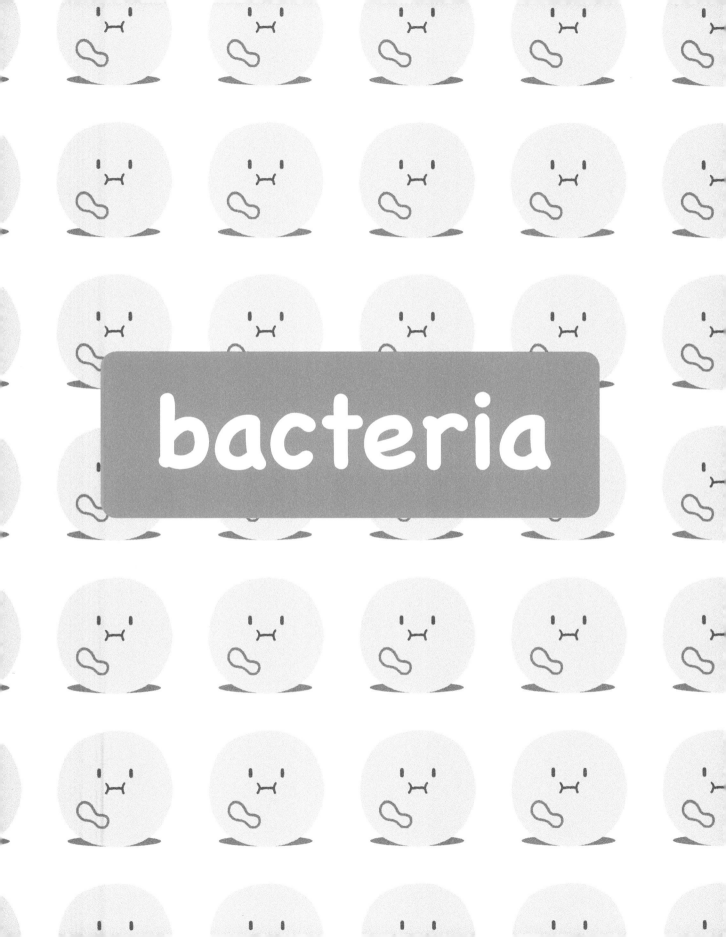

There are thousands of species of bacteria, which can be put into five groups according to their shape: spirilla (spiral), cocci (spherical), spirochaetes (corkscrew), vibrios (comma), and bacilli (rod).

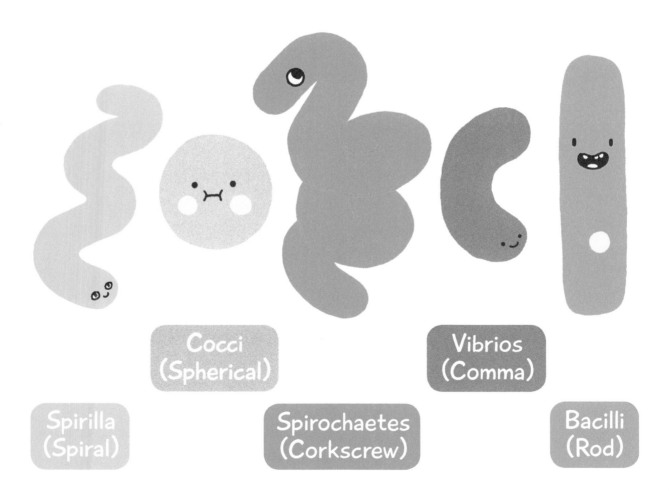

Spirilla (Spiral)

Cocci (Spherical)

Spirochaetes (Corkscrew)

Vibrios (Comma)

Bacilli (Rod)

Bacteria are single-celled organisms with no nucleus and most have no organelles with membranes around them. A bacteria's genetic material, or control centre, is contained in a single loop of DNA.

In one study, scientists swabbed **SIXTY BELLY BUTTONS** and identified **ONE THOUSAND FOUR HUNDRED AND FIFTY-EIGHT** new species of bacteria! One volunteer's belly button held bacteria that had only been found in soil from Japan, where the volunteer had never been!

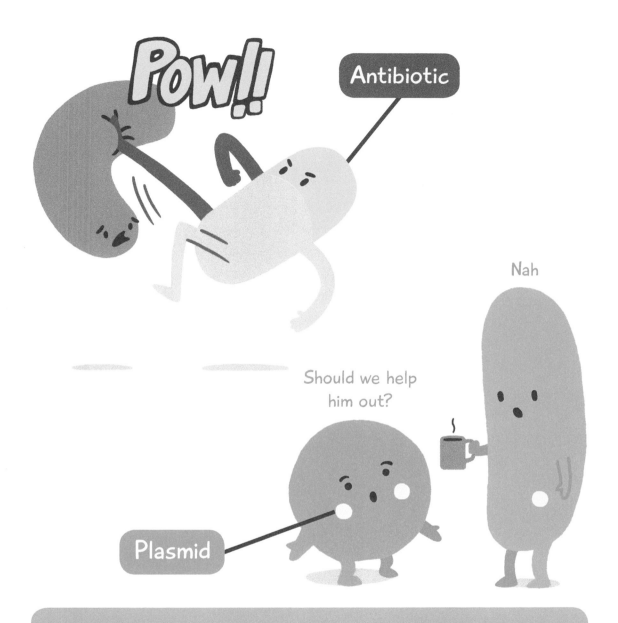

Some bacteria contain plasmids, which are small, circular molecules. Plasmids make a big difference to a bacterium's survival, such as helping it deal with stressful situations.

A medicinal problem facing today's world is the ability of harmful bacteria developing resistance to antibiotic drugs.

These bacteria transform to adapt to harsh environments or release enzymes. Enzymes are molecules that help with complex reactions, in this case, destroying antibiotics.

Treating a patient with antibiotics causes the microbes to adapt or die; this is known as "**SELECTIVE PRESSURE**". If a strain of bacteria acquires resistance to an antibiotic, it will survive the treatment. As the bacterial cell with acquired resistance multiplies, this resistance is passed on to its offspring.

Bacteria reproduce (create more life) through binary fission **"BI-NARY FISH-ON"**. This means that a cell can divide itself into two identical daughter cells.

The process begins with the DNA of the bacteria cell dividing into two replicas.

Next, the cell stretches and splits into two cells, each with its own identical strand of DNA.

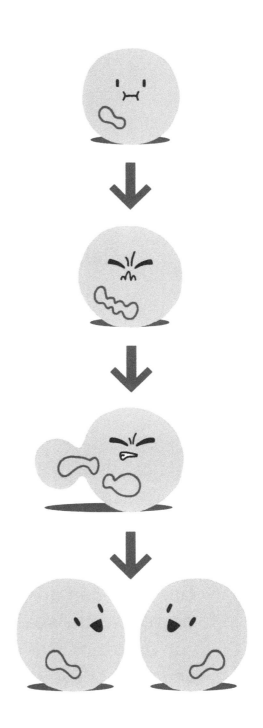

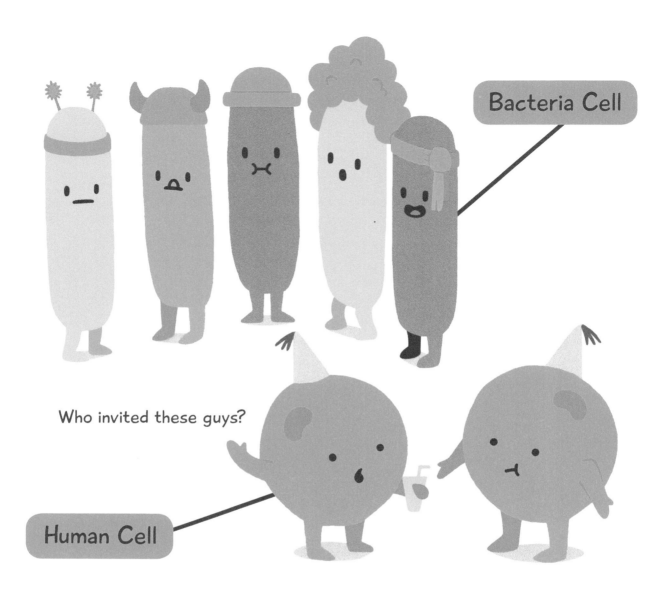

Bacteria can survive in a variety of habitats such as soil, rock, seas, and artic snow. Some exist in or on other living organisms such as plants and animals, **EVEN HUMANS!** In fact, there are roughly **TEN TIMES** the amount of bacteria cells to human cells in the human body.

Viruses are one of the **SMALLEST** and **DEADLIEST** of all the microbes. They can be found on and in just about every material and environment on Earth, so long as there are cells to infect.

Viruses can be passed by humans when shaking hands, or float through the air when someone sneezes. Make sure to **WASH YOUR HANDS** after you cough or sneeze, before handling food, and after you use the bathroom!

Viruses cause many diseases, some of which you might have already experienced, such as colds, flu, and chicken pox. Unfortunately, **ANTIBIOTICS CANNOT FIGHT VIRUSES** like they do on bacteria. However, scientists have created **VACCINES** that encourage our bodies to build immunity against certain viruses.

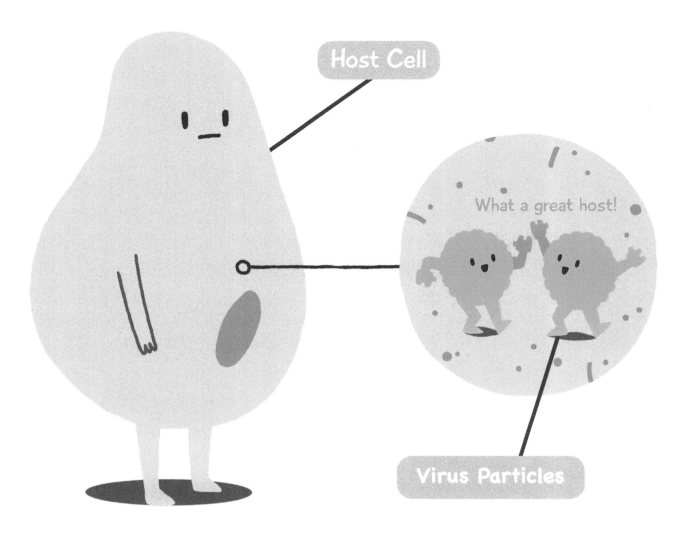

VIRUSES EXIST TO MAKE MORE VIRUSES.
They can only multiply inside the cells of other living organisms. The cell they multiply inside is called a host cell.

Initially, a virus attaches itself to a host cell through the use of a receptor. This can be likened to having a specific key for a specific lock.

Next, the virus or its genetic material enters the host cell. The virus **TAKES OVER** the host cell's reproductive machinery. It uses this to replicate the virus' control centre and build identical virus cells.

From one virus particle (called a viron), **MILLIONS** of virons are produced inside the host. They leave the host either through lysis **"LIE-SIS"** or budding.

Lysis is where virons burst out of the host cell — **OUCH!** When the virons are released they then go on to infect other host cells, and the same process continues.

Budding is where a virus leaves the host with parts of the host attached to it.

So what stops us from dropping dead when we're infected by a virus? Well, the human body is made up of **ONE HUNDRED TRILLION CELLS**, so in comparison to the cells in the human body, a million virons are like a raindrop in a bucket.

Also, our bodies are equipped with an immune system. Your immune system defends your body against infection and illness.

Immune System

When your immune system spots a viron, it will attempt to **DESTROY** it. Most of the time your immune system will work faster than a virus and stop it before it can seriously affect you.

Your immune system is made up of four major components: your skin; white blood cells; fluids in your mouth, nose, eyes and stomach; and your lymphatic system.

Virons

Your lymphatic system is a clear fluid that flows through your body. It **TRANSPORTS** fluid around cells and white blood cells to parts of the body where it is needed. It also carries bacteria and viruses to lymph nodes where they are **FILTERED AND DESTROYED**.

White blood cells play an important position in fighting bacteria and viruses. There are different kinds of white blood cells with distinct roles. For example, there are white blood cells that **SEEK OUT FOREIGN MATERIAL** (things that don't belong in your body), and other white blood cells that **KEEP AREAS OF YOUR BODY CLEAN**.

Fungi are single-celled organisms that can exist alone, like yeast cells, or as groups, known as multicellular clusters **"MUL-TI-CELL-U-LAR CLUS-TERS"** such as molds and mushrooms. They are mostly found living in soil or on plant material.

Multicellular filamentous molds **"MUL-TI-CELL-U-LAR- FIL-A-MEN-TOUS MOLDS"** are thread-like fungi. A single filament is called a hypha **"HI-FA"**. As the hyphae grow they form branches, which forms a network called a mycelium **"MY-CEL-IUM"**.

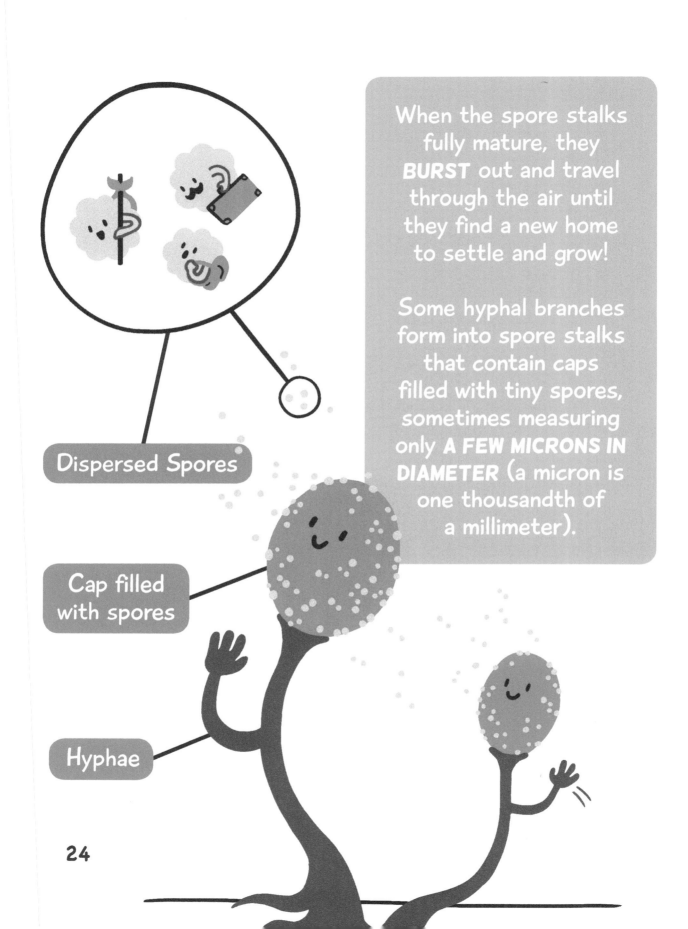

Dispersed Spores

Cap filled with spores

Hyphae

When the spore stalks fully mature, they **BURST** out and travel through the air until they find a new home to settle and grow!

Some hyphal branches form into spore stalks that contain caps filled with tiny spores, sometimes measuring only **A FEW MICRONS IN DIAMETER** (a micron is one thousandth of a millimeter).

24

Yeast cells are mostly lemon or egg shaped and typically grow in moist environments. They reproduce either by binary fission (duplicating themselves) or budding.

Reproducing through budding involves two parent yeast cells joining their daughter cells together.

Yeasts play an important role in the creation of bread and brewing beer. When yeasts "feed" on bread dough they **BREAK DOWN SUGARS AND PRODUCE CARBON DIOXIDE, WHICH MAKES THE DOUGH RISE.**

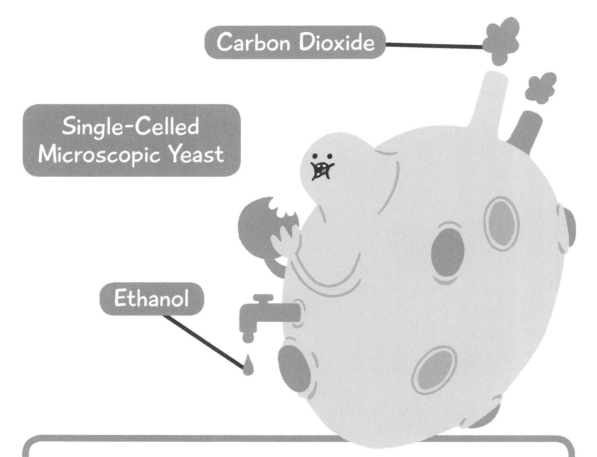

Carbon Dioxide

Single-Celled Microscopic Yeast

Ethanol

When yeast breaks down sugars to make beer, it produces the waste products carbon dioxide (which are the tiny air bubbles) and ethanol (alcohol).

Macroscopic filamentous fungi **"MAC-RO-SCOP-IC FIL-A-MEN-TOUS FUN-GUY"** form large fruiting bodies, often referred to as **MUSHROOMS OR TOADSTOOLS**.

The mushroom we see above ground is only part of the fungus, and this part is known as the fruiting body that hold spores.

This body is made up of tightly packed hyphae, which divide to create different parts of the fungal structure, such as the cap and stem.

Under the cap are gills that are covered in spores. A cap with a diameter of ten centimeters can produce up to **ONE HUNDRED MILLION SPORES PER HOUR**.

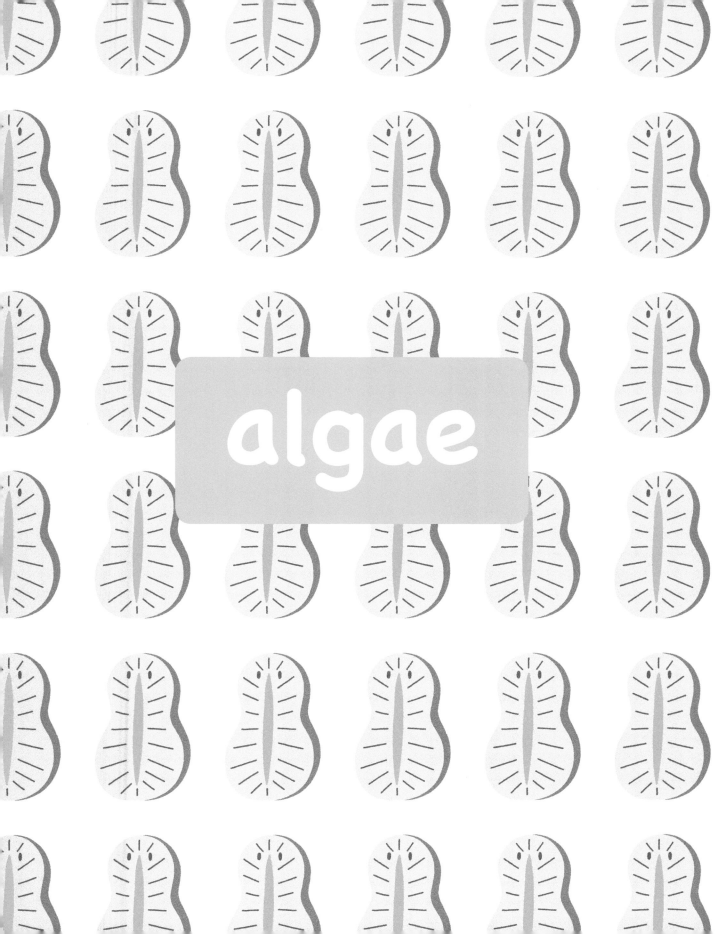

algae

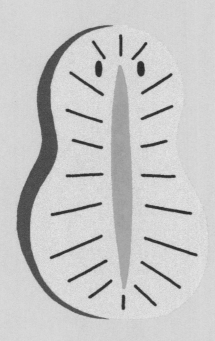

People often think of algae as seaweed or the slimy stuff in dirty swimming pools. However, there are many types of algae that can be found in a number of moist habitats such as soil, swamps, ponds, and aquatic plants.

Phytoplankton **"FHY-TO-PLANK-TON"**, also known as microalgae, float at the top of the ocean. Phytoplankton provide food for a variety of sea animals including whales, jellyfish, shrimp, and snails.

Algae play an important role in many ecosystems, including supporting the sea food chain, and creating about *SEVENTY PERCENT OF THE AIR WE BREATHE*!

Some algae can even be found on the **HAIRS OF SOUTH AMERICAN SLOTHS AND POLAR BEARS**! Other forms of algae partner with fungi to form lichens that can be found on rocky coasts and mountain summits.

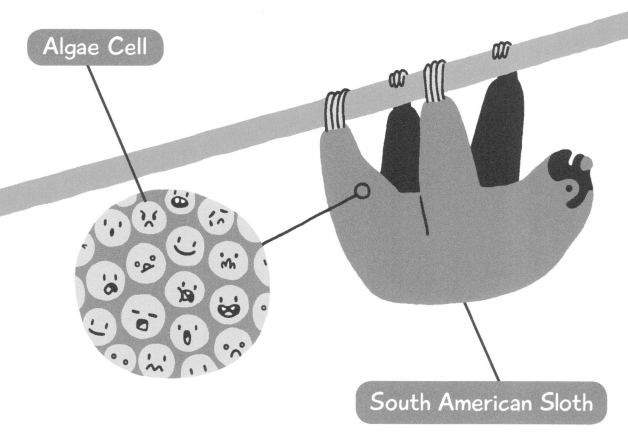

Algae Cell

South American Sloth

Some brown, yellow, and red algae can camouflage themselves green!

All algae contain the pigment chlorophyll, **"CLOR-O-FHIL"**, which is used to capture sunlight for photosynthesis **"FHO-TO-SIN-THE-SIS"**.

Algae get their colours (brown, yellow, or red) from pigments. Pigments are chemicals that reflect light. Some algae even have accessory pigments that camouflage themselves green!

Microscopic algae can exist as single cells, such as Chlamydomonas **"CLA-MID-O-MON-AS"**, or join together in chains like Spirogyra **"SPI-RO-JIE-RA"** or group together such as Rhodymenia **"RO-DE-MEAN-EE-A"**, also known as red seaweed.

Diatoms are a major group of microscopic algae: phytoplankton that live in both fresh and salt water. A unique feature of diatoms is their outer cell wall, called a frustule **"FRUSH-TULE"**. Frustules are mainly formed of silica.

Silica also exists inside us! It's in human connective tissues, bones, teeth, eyes, glands, organs, and skin. It is an essential ingredient of collagen, which helps keep our skin elastic and aids calcium to keep our bones strong.

When diatoms die, they sink. There, the soft area of their bodies decay and their silica cell wall remains. Over time the force of the water pushes silica together to form one giant layer. This is then mined, crushed, and used in polishes such as toothpaste and used in shoe boxes to absorb moisture.

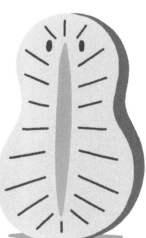

Or cat litter!

What will happen to us when we die?

Our silica coats will be used to absorb moisture in shoe boxes...

archaea

Archaea are among the earliest life forms on Earth and are thought to have existed for three to four billions of years!

Archaea are **TINY**, usually less than **ONE MICRON LONG**, which is **ONE ONE-THOUSANDTH OF A MILLIMETER**. Even under a high-power light microscope, the largest archaeans look like tiny dots.

They are single-celled microbes that have no nucleus or any other organelles inside their cells. Archaea look and act a lot like bacteria, so much so that before the late 1970s, scientists classified them as **WEIRD BACTERIA**!

Archaea are increasingly being valued in household products. Their enzymes (molecules that help with complex reactions) are sometimes called **EXTREMOZYMES**, which have been used in laundry detergent. This is because archaea are able to digest certain large molecules in hot or cold water, and in extremely alkaline environments, thus helping to remove life's little messes.

There are three main types of archaea:

Crenarchaeota **"KREN-ARE-KEY-OH-TA"** are grouped by their tolerance to extremes in temperature and acidity.

Euryarchaeota **"YOU-REE-ARE-KEY-OH-TA"** are methane producers and salt lovers — pass the soy sauce!

Korarchaeota **"CORE-ARE-KEY-OH-TA"** are a catch-all group about which very little is known.

Some subtypes of archaea include:

Thermophiles are categorised by their capacity to thrive in hot temperatures.

Halophiles are grouped by their ability to stand very salty environments.

Psychrophiles are those that survive in extremely cold temperatures.

Halophiles are grouped by their ability to stand very salty environments.

Halophile

Archaeans (as well as certain types of bacteria and eukaryotes) are the **ONLY LIVING ORGANISMS THAT CAN SURVIVE EXTREME HABITATS**, like hot springs or hypersaline water, which is very salty water.

However, archaeans are not limited to intense environments; recent research has shown them to **EXIST PRACTICALLY EVERYWHERE**. They have been found in plankton from open seas, ocean sediment, soil and **EVEN GUTS OF MAMMALS**!

Crenarchaeota can tolerate extremes in temperature and acidity.

Crenarchaeota

protozoa

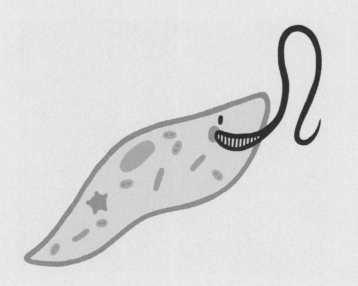

Protozoa means **"FIRST ANIMALS" OR "SMALL ANIMALS"** because they behave like tiny animals. For instance they hunt and gather other microbes as food. Protozoa mainly feed on bacteria, fungi, and other protozoa. Some absorb food through their cell tissues, others have mouth pores that sweep in food, whilst others surround food and engulf it.

One group of protozoa is the ciliates **"SILLY-ATES"** which are commonly known as the largest of the protozoa. Their average size is fifty micrometers, but they can be as large as **TWO MILLIMETERS**! That can be seen with the naked eye!

Ciliates have tiny hair-like structures called cilia that cover the outside of their body. They use this to move by beating the hairs in a continuous wave, a similar motion to oars.

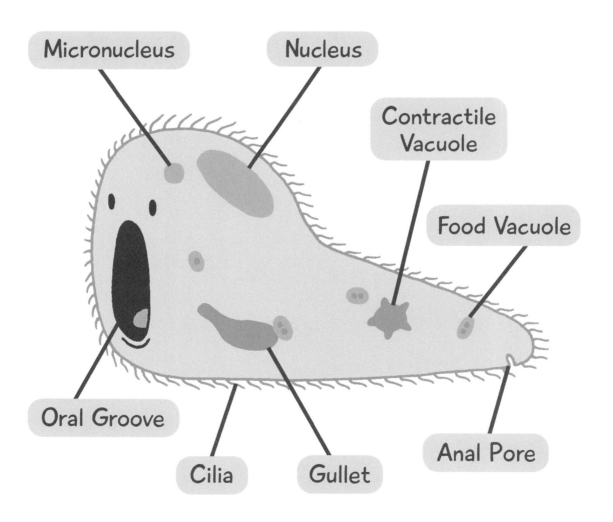

Micronucleus

Nucleus

Contractile Vacuole

Food Vacuole

Oral Groove

Cilia

Gullet

Anal Pore

A second group of protozoa is the flagellates **"FLAH-GEL-ETS"**, which are generally the smallest of the protozoa. Their sizes range from **FIVE TO TWENTY MICROMETERS**.

They contain one or several long thread-like structures, called a flagellum, which extend from the surface of the cell. Flagellates move their flagellum in a whip-like motion, which creates waves that propels the microbes around.

Flagellates contain one or several long thread-like structures, called a flagellum.

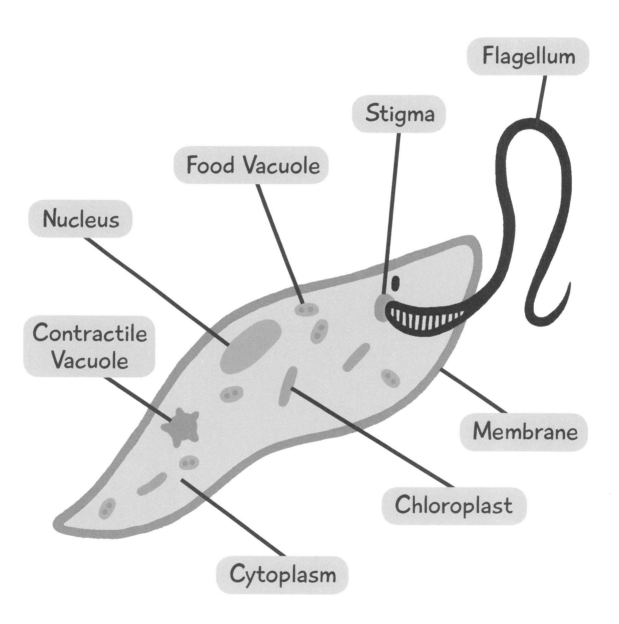

Flagellum

Stigma

Food Vacuole

Nucleus

Contractile Vacuole

Membrane

Chloroplast

Cytoplasm

The third group of protozoa is the amoebae **"AH-ME-BEE"**, which are microbes that move by stretching their cytoplasm, called pseudopods **"SUE-DOH-PODS"**, also known as "false feet".

These pseudopods can increase and decrease in size, a process called protoplasmic streaming **"PRO-TO-PLAS-MIC STREAM-ING"**. This allows ameobae to "chase" and surround their prey, followed by ingesting and absorbing the food.

One amoeba
"AH-ME-BA"

A group of amoebae
"AH-ME-BEE"

Amoebae travel by extending their cytoplasm

They feed on small organisms like bacteria and diatoms

terminology

BINARY FISSION **"BI-NARY FISH-ON"**	A method of reproduction within a cell that can divide itself into two identical daughter cells.
LYSIS **"LIE-SIS"**	A process in which a cell is broken down or destroyed.
BUDDING **"BUD-DING"**	Within viruses, the term *budding* is applied when the virus cell leaves the host cell with parts of the host attached to it.
MULTICELLULAR CLUSTERS **"MUL-TI-CELL-U-LAR CLUS-TERS"**	A group of single-celled organisms.
MULTICELLULAR FILAMENTOUS MOLDS **"MUL-TI-CELL-U-LAR FIL-A-MEN-TOUS MOLDS"**	Molds that are made up of very fine white filaments (hyphae).

MYCELIUM **"MY-CEL-IUM"**	A network of fine white filaments (hypahe).
MACROSCOPIC FILAMENTOUS FUNGI **"MAC-RO-SCOP-IC FIL-A-MEN-TOUS FUN-GUY"**	Large fruiting bodies often referred to as mushrooms or toadstools.
PHYTOPLANKTON **"FHY-TO-PLANK-TON"**	Also known as microscopic algae that float at the top of the ocean. They provide food for a variety of sea animals.
CHLOROPHYLL **"CLOR-O-FHIL"**	Chlorophyll is a green pigment, present in all green plants. It is responsible for the absorption of light to provide evergy for photosynthesis.
PHOTOSYNTHESIS **"FHO-TO-SIN-THE-SIS"**	The process of certain organisms (typically green plants) that use sunlight to create nutrients from carbon dioxide and water.

CHLAMYDOMONAS
"CLA-MID-O-MON-AS"

Microscopic single-celled algae.

SPIROGYRA
"SPI-RO-JIE-RA"

Chains of microscopic algae.

RHODYMENIA
"RO-DE-MEAN-EE-A"

Group of microscopic algae.

FRUSTULE
"FRUSH-TULE"

The outer cell of diatoms, mainly formed of silica.

CRENARCHAEOTA
"KREN-ARE-KEY-OH-TA"

A type of archaea. They can tolerate extremes in temperature and acidity.

EURYARCHAEOTA
"YOU-REE-ARE-KEY-OH-TA"

A type of archaea. They are methane producers and salt lovers.

KORARCHAEOTA
"CORE-ARE-KEY-OH-TA"

A catch-all group of archaea, which little is known.

CILIATES
"SILLY-ATES"

The largest group of protozoa. They have tiny hair-like structures that cover their bodies that they beat to propel them around.

FLAGELLATES
"FLAH-GEL-ETS"

Generally the smallest group of protozoa. They use one or several long thread-like structures to help them move.

AMOEBAE
"AH-ME-BEE"

A group of protozoa that move by stretching their cytoplasm called pseudopods.

PSEUDOPODS
"SUE-DOH-PODS"

Pseudopods (also known as "false feet") are extensions of an organism's cytoplasm. Amoebas alter the shape of pseudopods to move around in a crawl-like manner.

PROTOPLASMIC STREAMING
"PRO-TO-PLAS-MIC STREAM-ING"

Also known as cytoplasmic streaming, it is the fluid movement of the cytoplasm within a living organism. The motion transports nutrients, enzymes and larger particles within cells.

**GOODBYE FROM THE TEAM!
THEY HOPE TO SEE YOU SOON!**

BACTERIA

VIRUSES

FUNGI

ALGAE

ARCHAEA

PROTOZOA

CPSIA information can be obtained
at www.ICGtesting.com
Printed in the USA
LVHW06s0241250518
578479LV00014B/40/P